Your Financial Goals Workbook: Clarity, Control, and Confidence

Create a personalized plan to align your spending with your values and achieve your financial dreams.

Copyright & Permissions

Introduction

Welcome Message

Hi there! I'm so glad you're here, taking the first step toward gaining control over your finances. My name is Brittney Awad, and as an Accredited Financial Counselor, I know how overwhelming financial management can feel—especially when you don't know where to start. But with the right guidance and support, it's entirely possible to create a plan that reflects your values, helps you manage your spending, and leads to financial success. This workbook is designed to take the stress out of goal setting and help you break your financial goals into manageable, actionable steps.

Throughout this journey, remember that it's okay to go at your own pace. This workbook is your personal roadmap to not just managing money, but aligning it with what truly matters to you. You'll find space to set both short- and long-term goals, track your progress, and reflect on your habits. By the end, my hope is that you'll feel empowered and confident in your ability to shape your financial future.

Let's get started on this exciting path to financial freedom!

How to Use This Workbook

This workbook is designed to be your go-to tool for building and achieving your financial goals. Here's a simple guide to using it:

- Start with your goals: Begin by setting clear short-term and long-term financial goals. Don't worry about making them perfect—this section is all about getting your ideas down on paper.
- Break it down: In each section, you'll have the chance to break these goals into smaller, actionable steps. Focus on making these steps realistic and achievable.
- Track your progress: Use the savings goal trackers, habit challenges, and check-in pages to track how you're doing. Revisit these sections regularly to see how far you've come and make adjustments where needed.
- Reflect often: There's space throughout the workbook to reflect on your progress and financial habits. Use these sections to review your mindset and see how your money management is aligning with your values.

Take it one section at a time, and remember—this workbook is yours to use however best supports you. Come back to it regularly to adjust your goals, track your progress, and celebrate your wins. You've got this!

You can access free copies of the charts and worksheets in this workbook on myfinancialequity.com.

Table of Contents

Section 1: Clarify Your Values and Vision

Activity: Identify Your Core Values

Understanding your core values is essential for aligning your financial goals with what truly matters to you. Take a moment to reflect on the following prompts:

- **What do you value most in life?** (Consider aspects like family, education, security, travel, health, etc.)
- **How would you like your finances to support these values?** (Think about how your financial decisions can enhance your priorities and values.)

Space for Reflection:

_____

_____

_____

_____

_____

_____

_____

_____

Activity: Create Your Financial Vision

Now that you've identified your core values, it's time to picture the future you want your finances to support. This vision will act as your "why" when making financial decisions.

Take a few minutes to reflect on the following prompts. Don't overthink it—just write what feels true to you.

- Imagine your life five to ten years from now. What does it look like? Where are you living, working, or traveling?
- How does your financial situation feel in this vision? (Consider words like secure, free, generous, independent, stable, adventurous.)
- What goals have you achieved that make you proud? (Think about debt you've paid off, savings you've built, or milestones like buying a home, starting a business, or taking a dream trip.)
- How does this vision connect back to the values you wrote about earlier?

Space for Reflection:

Use the space below to describe your vision in detail. Write as if it has already happened—for example, "I am debt-free and saving for a home that feels safe and welcoming," rather than "I want to be debt-free." Writing in the present tense helps your brain start to see this future as possible.

_____

_____

_____

_____

_____

Section 2: Set SMART Financial Goals

What Are SMART Goals?
Setting SMART goals is a powerful way to turn your financial dreams into reality. SMART stands for:
- **Specific:** Clearly define what you want to achieve.
- **Measurable:** Quantify your goals to track your progress.
- **Achievable:** Ensure your goal is realistic and attainable.
- **Relevant:** Align your goals with your values and long-term aspirations.
- **Time-bound:** Set a deadline to stay on track.

Example 1: Emergency Fund
Goal: "I will save $500 in the next 3 months for an emergency fund by setting aside $50 from each paycheck."
- **Specific:** Clear focus on saving for an emergency fund.
- **Measurable:** Save $500 in 3 months.
- **Achievable:** Setting aside $50 per paycheck is realistic.
- **Relevant:** Supports the value of financial security.
- **Time-bound:** 3-month deadline helps you stay focused and committed.

Example 2: Paying Off Credit Card Debt
Goal: "I will pay off $1,200 in credit card debt within the next 6 months by making monthly payments of $200."
- **Specific:** Targeting credit card debt repayment.
- **Measurable:** Total debt of $1,200 with monthly payments.
- **Achievable:** $200 per month works for this example.
- **Relevant:** Improves financial health and reduces stress.
- **Time-bound:** 6-month timeframe provides structure.

Example 3: Saving for a Vacation
Goal: "I will save $1,000 for a vacation in 12 months by setting aside $85 from each paycheck."
- **Specific:** Focus on saving for a vacation.
- **Measurable:** Goal of $1,000 over 12 months.
- **Achievable:** $85 per paycheck is a feasible amount.
- **Relevant:** Aligns with self-care and enjoyment values.
- **Time-bound:** 12-month period for planning and anticipation.

SMART Goal Worksheets

Use the space below to write down your financial goals for different timeframes. Be sure to think about what is most important to you!

Short-Term Goals (within 1 year):

1.	
2.	
3.	

Mid-Term Goals (1-5 years):

1.	
2.	
3.	

Long-Term Goals (5+ years):

1.	
2.	
3.	

Section 3: Break Down Your Goals Into Actionable Steps

Goal Breakdown Template

Breaking down your financial goals into specific, actionable steps is crucial for turning your dreams into reality. This process not only makes your goals more manageable but also helps you stay motivated and accountable. Follow the instructions below to outline your goals and the actions needed to achieve them.

1) Define Your Goal:
- Begin by clearly writing down your financial goal. Be specific about what you want to achieve and set a realistic timeframe. For example, instead of saying, "I want to save money," specify, "I want to save $500 for an emergency fund in 3 months."

2) Identify Necessary Actions:
- Next, think about the specific actions you need to take to reach this goal. Consider breaking your actions down into smaller, manageable tasks. Here are some prompts to help you identify your steps:
  - **Calculate Savings Per Paycheck:** Determine how much money you need to set aside from each paycheck to reach your goal by the deadline.
  - **Set Up Automatic Transfers:** Consider setting up automatic transfers to a dedicated savings account to make saving easier and more consistent.
  - **Adjust Spending Habits:** Identify areas where you can cut back on non-essential spending. This could be dining out less or canceling unused subscriptions.
  - **Monitor Your Progress:** Decide how you will track your savings progress (e.g., using a spreadsheet, app, or journal).

3) Prioritize Your Actions:

- o Once you've listed your actions, prioritize them. Determine which steps are most critical to achieving your goal and tackle those first. This helps you focus your efforts where they will have the most impact.

4) Review and Adjust:

- o As you begin to implement your plan, regularly review your progress and be willing to adjust your actions as needed. Life can be unpredictable, so it's essential to remain flexible and adapt your approach if circumstances change.

Weekly Progress Tracker:

Use this weekly tracker to mark your progress on the specific actions you listed above. Checking in weekly will help you stay accountable and make adjustments as needed.

- **What to track each week:**
  - o Did you set aside the planned amount of money?
  - o Have you automated transfers or cut down on unnecessary spending?
  - o Are you consistently following through on each action?
- **How to use the tracker:**
  - o At the end of each week, note whether or not you completed each action. If not, reflect on what may have caused setbacks and adjust your actions for the next week. Use a simple Yes/No checklist for each step.

Week	Action 1 (e.g., Calculate savings per paycheck)	Action 2 (e.g., Set up automatic transfers)	Action 3 (e.g., Cut non-essential spending)	Notes
Week 1	[ ] Yes [ ] No	[ ] Yes [ ] No	[ ] Yes [ ] No	

Week	Action 1 (e.g., Calculate savings per paycheck)	Action 2 (e.g., Set up automatic transfers)	Action 3 (e.g., Cut non-essential spending)	Notes
Week 2	[ ] Yes [ ] No	[ ] Yes [ ] No	[ ] Yes [ ] No	
Week 3	[ ] Yes [ ] No	[ ] Yes [ ] No	[ ] Yes [ ] No	
Week 4	[ ] Yes [ ] No	[ ] Yes [ ] No	[ ] Yes [ ] No	

Monthly Progress Tracker:
The monthly tracker is where you'll see bigger-picture progress. You can summarize how much you've saved, the changes in your spending habits, and whether you're getting closer to your goal.
- **What to track each month:**
  - Total savings toward your goal.
  - Successes in cutting non-essential spending.
  - Adjustments you've made to stay on track.
  - Any new insights or challenges.
  - Are you consistently following through on each action?
- **How to use the tracker:**
  - At the end of each month, take some time to review your progress. Reflect on what's working and what isn't. You can adjust your goals or actions if you need to, but celebrate your wins along the way.

Month	Total Savings Toward Goal	Notes

Month	Total Savings Toward Goal	Notes

Section 4: Build Better Financial Habits

Introduction
Building strong financial habits is key to staying on track with your spending plan and financial goals. This section will help you implement daily, weekly, and monthly habits that support your progress. The goal is to make these habits second nature so that they contribute to your long-term financial success.

Habit Tracker

Instructions: Use this habit tracker to monitor your progress over the next 30 days. Choose a few key habits to focus on, like tracking expenses, setting aside money for savings, or scheduling a "money date" with yourself to review your finances. Check in daily to build consistency and reflect on your progress.

Example Habits:
- **Track expenses daily:** Log every purchase to understand your spending habits better.
- **Review spending weekly:** Set aside time each week to analyze and adjust.
- **Add to savings weekly:** Make consistent progress toward your financial goals.
- **Set financial boundaries:** Evaluate your needs versus wants before buying.

How to Use:
1. Select three habits that are most relevant to your financial goals.
2. Track them daily for 30 days using the chart. Mark your progress and reflect.
3. At the end of each week, evaluate which habits are becoming easier and where you still need to focus.

_____

_____

_____

Day	Habit 1	Habit 2	Habit 3	Notes (Challenges/Successes)
1	Yes / No	Yes / No	Yes / No	
2	Yes / No	Yes / No	Yes / No	
3	Yes / No	Yes / No	Yes / No	
4	Yes / No	Yes / No	Yes / No	
5	Yes / No	Yes / No	Yes / No	
6	Yes / No	Yes / No	Yes / No	
7	Yes / No	Yes / No	Yes / No	
8	Yes / No	Yes / No	Yes / No	
9	Yes / No	Yes / No	Yes / No	
10	Yes / No	Yes / No	Yes / No	
11	Yes / No	Yes / No	Yes / No	
12	Yes / No	Yes / No	Yes / No	
13	Yes / No	Yes / No	Yes / No	
14	Yes / No	Yes / No	Yes / No	
15	Yes / No	Yes / No	Yes / No	

Day	Habit 1	Habit 2	Habit 3	Notes (Challenges/Successes)
16	Yes / No	Yes / No	Yes / No	
17	Yes / No	Yes / No	Yes / No	
18	Yes / No	Yes / No	Yes / No	
19	Yes / No	Yes / No	Yes / No	
20	Yes / No	Yes / No	Yes / No	
21	Yes / No	Yes / No	Yes / No	
22	Yes / No	Yes / No	Yes / No	
23	Yes / No	Yes / No	Yes / No	
24	Yes / No	Yes / No	Yes / No	
25	Yes / No	Yes / No	Yes / No	
26	Yes / No	Yes / No	Yes / No	
27	Yes / No	Yes / No	Yes / No	
28	Yes / No	Yes / No	Yes / No	
29	Yes / No	Yes / No	Yes / No	
30	Yes / No	Yes / No	Yes / No	

30-Day No-Spend Challenge Tracker

This chart will help you track your success in avoiding non-essential spending over a month.

Instructions for the No-Spend Challenge Tracker:

- For the next 30 days, aim to avoid any non-essential spending.
- Each day, check off **Yes** or **No** to indicate if you succeeded in avoiding non-essential purchases.
- Use the **Notes** section to document any challenges or insights regarding temptations and how you felt about your spending habits.
- At the end of each week, reflect on your progress with the following questions:
  - What were your biggest temptations this week?
  - How much money did you save?
  - What did you learn about your spending habits?

Day	Did You Avoid Non-Essential Spending?	Notes
Day 1	[ ] Yes / [ ] No	
Day 2	[ ] Yes / [ ] No	
Day 3	[ ] Yes / [ ] No	
Day 4	[ ] Yes / [ ] No	
Day 5	[ ] Yes / [ ] No	
Day 6	[ ] Yes / [ ] No	
Day 7	[ ] Yes / [ ] No	
Day 8	[ ] Yes / [ ] No	
Day 9	[ ] Yes / [ ] No	
Day 10	[ ] Yes / [ ] No	
Day 11	[ ] Yes / [ ] No	

Day	Did You Avoid Non-Essential Spending?	Notes
Day 12	[ ] Yes / [ ] No	
Day 13	[ ] Yes / [ ] No	
Day 14	[ ] Yes / [ ] No	
Day 15	[ ] Yes / [ ] No	
Day 16	[ ] Yes / [ ] No	
Day 17	[ ] Yes / [ ] No	
Day 18	[ ] Yes / [ ] No	
Day 19	[ ] Yes / [ ] No	
Day 20	[ ] Yes / [ ] No	
Day 21	[ ] Yes / [ ] No	
Day 22	[ ] Yes / [ ] No	
Day 23	[ ] Yes / [ ] No	
Day 24	[ ] Yes / [ ] No	
Day 25	[ ] Yes / [ ] No	
Day 26	[ ] Yes / [ ] No	
Day 27	[ ] Yes / [ ] No	
Day 28	[ ] Yes / [ ] No	
Day 29	[ ] Yes / [ ] No	
Day 30	[ ] Yes / [ ] No	

Section 5: Create a Spending Plan Aligned with Your Goals

Introduction to Spending Plans
A spending plan is a flexible, intentional approach to managing your money. Unlike a strict budget, which can feel limiting, a spending plan focuses on aligning your spending with your priorities and values. It helps you make thoughtful decisions about where to allocate, save, and cut back, all while supporting your financial goals. Think of it as a dynamic guide that evolves with your circumstances, keeping you on track.

Activity: Track Your Current Spending
Before creating a spending plan, it's essential to understand where your money is currently going. Use the worksheet on the next page to track your spending for a month. This activity will help you categorize your expenses and reflect on how your spending aligns (or doesn't) with your goals and values.

There are two ways to complete this activity.
- The first way is by tracking your spending every day for a month.
- The second way is to review all of your statements - including for your checking account(s), savings account(s), and credit card(s).

Three months of tracking spending is preferable to get the clearest picture of your personal finances.

Questions to Consider:
- Where is your money going?
- Does your spending align with your financial goals and values?

Category	Amount Spent	Notes
Necessities		
Discretionary Spending		
Savings		

Take time to analyze these categories at the end of the month and reflect on any spending habits that surprise you or don't align with your goals.

Income Categories	Estimated Amount	Actual Amount	Difference
Regular Hours			
Overtime			
Other Income			
Total Income			

Expense Categories	Estimated Amount	Actual Amount	Difference
Rent/Mortgage			
Utilities			
Phone Bill			
Wifi			
Car Insurance			
Car Payment			
Gas			
Groceries			
Eating Out			
Insurance Copays			
Savings			
Investments			
Entertainment			
Child Care			
Total Expenses			
Remaining Balance			

Use the blank lines for anything specific to your budget. You can also find a free Google Sheet on myfinancialequity.com to use for budgeting, including templates for weekly, bi-weekly, and monthly budgets.

Create a Simple Spending Plan

Now that you've tracked your current spending, let's create a spending plan that aligns with your goals. Follow these steps:

1) List Your Income: Write down all sources of income (e.g., salary, side jobs, passive income).

2) List Necessary Expenses: Include essentials like rent, utilities, groceries, and transportation.

3) Allocate Money Toward Savings and Goals: Make sure to prioritize savings and any specific financial goals you have.

4) Plan for Discretionary Spending: Allow room for non-essential spending, but keep it in balance with your goals.

Tips for Using the Spending Plan Chart

1) Be Realistic: When estimating amounts, consider past spending habits and upcoming expenses. Accuracy will help you set achievable goals.

2) Track Regularly: Update the Actual Amount column weekly or monthly to see how well you're sticking to your plan. Regular tracking will help you identify patterns in your spending.

3) Set Specific Goals: In the Goal column, write down specific financial goals for each category, such as saving for a vacation or reducing dining out expenses. This will give you a clear target to aim for.

4) Reflect and Adjust: At the end of each month, review your spending plan. Reflect on what worked, what didn't, and adjust your estimates and goals as needed. Flexibility is key to staying on track.

5) Celebrate Small Wins: Acknowledge any progress, even if it's minor. Celebrating small victories can motivate you to stick with your spending plan.

6) Use Categories Wisely: Ensure the expense categories reflect your priorities and values. If something is essential to your lifestyle, allocate appropriate funds to it.

7) Seek Help if Needed: If you find it challenging to stick to your spending plan, consider reaching out for guidance or support. Financial counseling can provide additional strategies and accountability.

Income Sources	Estimated Amount	Actual Amount	Goal
Salary			
Side Hustle			
Other Income			
Total Income			

Expense Categories	Estimated Amount	Actual Amount	Goal
Rent/Mortgage			
Utilities			
Transportation			
Food			
Insurance			
Savings & Investments			
Entertainment			
Dining Out			
Total Expenses			
Remaining Balance			

Reflection Questions

As you work on your spending plan, take a moment to reflect on these questions. They will help you evaluate your financial priorities and identify areas for improvement:

How can you adjust your spending to align more with your goals?

- Consider what changes you can make in your spending habits to better support your financial objectives. Are there specific expenses you can reduce or eliminate to free up funds for your goals?

_____

_____

_____

_____

_____

Are there areas where you can cut back?

- Think about your current spending categories. Are there discretionary expenses or non-essential items that you could reduce? Identifying these areas will help you create more room in your budget for savings and goals.

_____

_____

_____

_____

_____

Take your time to answer these questions thoroughly, as they will guide your financial decisions and strengthen your commitment to your spending plan.

Section 6: Monthly Financial Check-In

Monthly Review Template
This monthly review template is designed to help you reflect on your financial progress, identify areas for improvement, and celebrate your successes. Taking time at the end of each month to review your financial habits not only keeps you accountable and motivated but also helps you plan for the upcoming month. This proactive approach ensures you stay on track toward your financial goals.

Instructions:
At the end of each month, take a moment to fill out this review template. Reflect on your wins and challenges, and use the insights gained to make adjustments for the upcoming month.

Wins This Month	Challenges This Month	Adjustments for Next Month
1.	1.	1.
2.	2.	2.
3.	3.	3.

Reflection Questions:
1. What did you do well this month?
2. Were there any unexpected expenses or challenges?
3. How did your spending align with your goals?
4. What specific adjustments will you make for next month?

Notes:
- Consider discussing your financial review with a trusted friend or family member for added accountability.
- Use this template monthly to track your progress and adapt your strategies as needed.

_____

_____

_____

_____

_____

_____

_____

_____

_____

_____

Section 7: Reflect and Celebrate Your Progress

Reflecting on your financial journey is crucial for recognizing how far you've come and identifying areas for continued growth. Taking the time to celebrate your progress helps reinforce positive behaviors and keeps you motivated.

Annual Financial Reflection
At the end of the year, set aside time to reflect on your financial achievements and lessons learned. Use the prompts below to guide your reflection.

Reflection Prompts:
- What financial goals did you achieve this year?

- What were your biggest financial lessons?

- In what areas did you feel the most successful?

- What challenges did you face, and how did you overcome them?

- What new financial habits did you develop?

Celebrating Wins

Recognizing your successes is just as important as evaluating your challenges. Celebrating your wins can motivate you to keep pushing forward. Here are some ideas for how to celebrate your progress:

Plan a Small Treat: Allow yourself a budget-friendly reward for your hard work, like a special dessert, a new book, or a movie night at home.

Share Your Success: Talk about your achievements with a friend or family member who will celebrate with you. Create a supportive environment where everyone shares their wins.

Create a Vision Board: Visualize your goals and dreams for the upcoming year as a way to stay inspired. Include images, quotes, and anything that represents what you're aiming for.

Host a Small Celebration: Invite friends or family over for a casual get-together to celebrate your financial achievements. Share your journey and inspire others.

Start a Gratitude Jar: Write down your financial wins and lessons learned on slips of paper and place them in a jar. At the end of the year, read through them to reflect on your progress.

Invest in Your Growth: Consider using part of your savings to attend a workshop, buy a book, or enroll in a course that can help you further your financial knowledge.

Reward Yourself with Experiences: Treat yourself to an activity you enjoy, like a day trip, a spa day, or a hobby class. Investing in experiences can enhance your well-being and provide lasting memories.

Celebrating Wins

Recognizing your successes is just as important as evaluating your challenges. Celebrating your wins can motivate you to keep pushing forward. Here are some ideas for how to celebrate your progress:

Set New Goals: Use your success as motivation to set a new financial goal for the upcoming year. This will keep the momentum going and help you continue building on your progress.

Journal Your Journey: Write a brief reflection on your financial journey throughout the year. Document what you learned, the challenges you overcame, and how you've grown.

Create a Success Playlist: Curate a playlist of songs that make you feel empowered and motivated. Play this music whenever you need a boost or when celebrating your wins.

Visual Reminders: Create visual reminders of your goals and achievements. Use sticky notes, posters, or digital wallpapers that keep your successes front and center.

Connect with a Mentor: Reach out to someone you admire in the financial world. Share your wins and ask for advice on your next steps. Their perspective can be valuable and encouraging.

Reflect on Your Journey: Take some time to sit quietly and reflect on how far you've come. Consider writing a letter to yourself acknowledging your accomplishments and growth.

Explore New Opportunities: Use your achievements as a launchpad to explore new financial opportunities, such as researching investments, savings accounts, or side hustles that align with your goals.

Resources & Tips

In your journey toward better financial health, having access to reliable resources and practical tips can make all the difference. This section provides a curated list of tools, websites, and strategies to support you as you continue to build and maintain your financial habits.

Practical Tips for Success

1) **Set Specific Goals:** Clearly define your financial goals to stay focused and motivated. Break larger goals into smaller, actionable steps.

2) **Track Your Progress:** Regularly review your spending and savings. Use budgeting apps or spreadsheets to visualize your progress.

3) **Automate Savings:** Set up automatic transfers to your savings account. Consider high-yield savings accounts for better returns.

4) **Limit Impulse Purchases:** Create a waiting period for non-essential purchases to avoid buyer's remorse.

5) **Practice Mindfulness:** Be aware of your spending triggers and emotional responses to money. Reflect on how they affect your habits.

6) **Educate Yourself:** Continuously seek knowledge through books, podcasts, or online courses. The more informed you are, the better decisions you can make.

7) **Utilize Community Resources:** Check local community centers for free financial workshops or seminars that offer valuable resources.

8) **Reflect and Adjust:** Take time each month to reflect on your financial journey. Celebrate successes and reassess your goals to keep plans aligned.

Community Support

Consider joining a financial support group. Sharing experiences can provide valuable insights and accountability. Engage with your community by:

- **Participating in Online Forums:** Websites like Reddit offer advice and support from others facing similar challenges.
- **Finding an Accountability Partner:** Share your goals with a friend or family member for regular check-ins to stay motivated.

Helpful Resources
Note: Underlined items are clickable.

- **Budgeting Apps:**
  - **Monarch Money:** A user-friendly app for tracking expenses, creating budgets, and setting financial goals. It offers collaborative features for family or shared finances.
  - **You Need a Budget (YNAB):** An interactive tool that focuses on helping you allocate every dollar to your expenses and savings goals, promoting proactive financial management.
- **Debt Payoff Resources:**
  - **PowerPay from Utah State University:** provides multiple options for debt payoff so you can find the one that works for you; https://extension.usu.edu/powerpay/
- **Financial Education Websites:**
  - **Consumer Financial Protection Bureau (CFPB):** Provides information on a variety of financial topics, including budgeting, saving, and credit management.
  - **National Endowment for Financial Education (NEFE):** Offers free resources and educational materials on personal finance topics.
- **Personal Finance Blogs:**
  - **Investopedia:** A comprehensive resource for financial education, offering articles on a wide range of topics, from basic budgeting to investing strategies.
  - **NerdWallet:** Provides tools and advice for comparing financial products, budgeting, and managing money effectively.
- **Books:**
  - **"The Psychology of Money" by Morgan Housel:** Explores how emotions and behavior influence financial decisions, offering valuable insights into wealth-building.
  - **"Financial Freedom" by Grant Sabatier:** Offers a practical guide to achieving financial independence through smart money management, investing, and maximizing your income.

Helpful Resources
Note: Underlined items are clickable.

- **Podcasts:**
  - **"Bad with Money":** Hosted by Gabe Dunn, this podcast features authentic discussions about financial mishaps and practical advice aimed at helping listeners avoid common money mistakes.
  - **"BiggerPockets Podcast":** Focuses on personal finance and real estate investing, featuring guests who share their financial journeys and strategies for building financial security.
- **Professional Support:**
  - Seek guidance from accredited financial counselors who can provide personalized advice tailored to your unique financial situation. Look for local counselors or search for resources through the Association for Financial Counseling & Planning Education (AFCPE).

Moving Forward

As you wrap up this workbook, remember that the journey to financial empowerment is ongoing. The insights and strategies you've learned here are stepping stones toward achieving your financial goals.

Here are some key takeaways to keep in mind as you move forward:

1. **Embrace Continuous Learning:** Financial literacy is a lifelong journey. Continue to explore resources, attend workshops, and seek advice to enhance your understanding.
2. **Set Clear Goals:** Regularly review and adjust your financial goals to ensure they align with your values and aspirations.
3. **Take Small Steps:** Remember that progress doesn't have to be drastic. Small, consistent steps can lead to significant changes over time. Focus on one habit or goal at a time.
4. **Breathe Deep:** Finances can be stressful, and it's essential to practice self-care. When feeling overwhelmed, take a moment to breathe deeply and refocus. A clear mind can lead to better decision-making.
5. **Celebrate Progress:** Take time to acknowledge your achievements, no matter how small. Every step forward is worth celebrating!
6. **Stay Accountable:** Share your goals and progress with a trusted friend or family member. Having support can help you stay motivated and focused.
7. **Revisit This Workbook:** Keep this workbook handy as a resource to guide you whenever you need a refresher or a boost in your financial journey.

Affiliate Disclosure: Some resources mentioned in this workbook contain affiliate links. By purchasing through these links, you are supporting my work at no additional cost to you. Thank you for your support!

www.ingramcontent.com/pod-product-compliance
Lightning Source LLC
Chambersburg PA
CBHW071533210326
41597CB00018B/2980